SEEING GOD

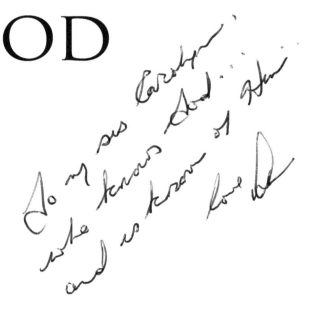

DAN THIESSEN

ISBN 978-1-64258-733-3 (paperback)
ISBN 978-1-64258-734-0 (digital)

Copyright © 2018 by Dan Thiessen

All rights reserved. No part of this publication may be reproduced, distributed, or transmitted in any form or by any means, including photocopying, recording, or other electronic or mechanical methods without the prior written permission of the publisher. For permission requests, solicit the publisher via the address below.

Christian Faith Publishing, Inc.
832 Park Avenue
Meadville, PA 16335
www.christianfaithpublishing.com

Scriptures taken from the Holy Bible, New International Version®, NIV®. Copyright © 1973, 1978, 1984, 2011 by Biblica, Inc.™ Used by permission of Zondervan. All rights reserved worldwide. www.zondervan.com.

The "NIV" and "New International Version" are trademarks registered in the United States Patent and Trademark Office by Biblica, Inc.™

Printed in the United States of America

TESTIMONIES
(Following a "Seeing God" Seminar)

Today I learned just how much God loves me and the characteristics of God to help me know Him better.
—Darlene

I recently attended a seminar hosted by Dan Thiessen of Father's Heart Ministries. Although I am a Christian and desperately want a relationship with God, I have always subconsciously viewed God as an angry parent, ready to chastise or even destroy at any moment. My mind has always restricted the words "God is love" to mean, "For God so loved the world…" and that's it—to me these words had no bearing on the "here and now." Dan's seminar has set me on a new journey of discovery (I don't have all the answers yet, but it's OK), making me realize just how patient God is, and how much He wants a relationship with a "wild flower, who is here today and gone tomorrow."
—Henri

Today, I learned a "no-doubt" way to discern judgment on me, and where it is from— when it is my Father in Heaven wanting my attention, to steer me correctly, or if it is not of Him and of a condemning evil. And I will continue to rebuke any condemnation that comes to me, or others.
—Mary Pat

INTRODUCTION

I was going to ask you to close your eyes for an illustration to get this book going but then realized you wouldn't be able to read what to do next. My bad. So here's the deal, please read the instructions, *then* close your eyes. Sound fair?

Here we go. Imagine yourself in a room with no one else there (alone, in other words!). You are quite comfortable. You might even be writing or drawing something as you are alone with your thoughts.

Suddenly you are interrupted by the door behind you being jostled and someone entering the room. You turn to see who it is and are quite shocked to see it is God.

What do you do? How do you react?

Do you stay standing there, run toward Him, or run away from Him? Do you approach Him, fall at His feet crying, or gaze into His eyes while smiling? Is there laughter or remorse? Do you dance, or are you frozen where you stand? Do you feel guilt or freedom? Fear or relief?

Take a moment and write down your reaction. Don't stop to think. Just jot down your immediate response. Listen to your heart, your instincts. If you think too much, you might try to analyze and thus defeat the purpose of this illustration.

There are so many ways to react in this situation. And these reactions change over time depending on where we are in our relationship with God.

What you felt as you read this illustration for the first time might be different once you finish reading this book and see God once again, only this time through a different set of eyes.

How you see God affects so many things. It is at the core of our relationship with Him. My thinking as I started this project was, "Who we perceive God to be determines how close we get to Him."

If I could somehow, and in some way affect a person's view of God positively, maybe, just maybe they would draw closer and have the dynamic relationship with God He has desired all along.

See if you identify at all with these lyrics to a song I wrote:

That's Who You Are
Dan Thiessen © 2007

VERSE ONE:
Who do I think You are?
What do I think You're like?
Do I think You're always angry?
While You're watching over me
How do I think You sound?
When judgmental thoughts abound
God, I really want to know You
For who You are, not who I think You to be

CHORUS:
You are a shelter when it's raining,
You are a strength when all is draining
You're a rock and shield and refuge
That will never change,
'cause that's who You are

VERSE TWO:
Where did I go so wrong?
What came and changed my song?
God, I think I've been distracted,
I've let my feelings take control
I'm coming back to You.
With all that I say and do
Show me Your face, Lord
I want to be changed by all that You are

We, as humans, tend to complicate things. I'm writing this book to get us back to the basics. Though what I am saying is theologically sound, you will not be inundated with theology, just simple thoughts to help you draw closer to the God who loved you so much, He sent His son to die for you.

I'd ask you to take a moment right here and write out a prayer. What are you looking for as you read this book? What is at the core of your heart with regard to your relationship with God? Some of you might not be used to this, but it is worth a shot. What this will do is articulate your thoughts and intents.

I once wrote the following prayer:

> Dear Abba Father, it has been such a long time since I have felt son-ship, that true sense of belonging. For so long I have felt I have been on my own and that You have been just checking in from time to time.
>
> I want son-ship. I do not want independence. I want affection and not distance. I want intimacy and not ambivalence. When You call, touch my shoulder so that I know You are close.
>
> When You are near, let me know You are near. Talk to me when I am not paying attention so that I will pay attention. I crave a son-ship that is undeserved and yet freely given.
>
> Stand shoulder to shoulder with me and see the view from my eyes. I want son-ship so bad there's nothing I wouldn't sacrifice to obtain it.
>
> Be my Father, my Abba Father, and I will be Your son.
>
> Dan

What I'd like you to do next might be even more difficult, but I'd ask you to at least try. Take another moment to go to your quiet place, the place where you listen best. Now I'd ask you to write out God's response to your prayer.

When I wrote the above prayer, the following is what I heard from God in response:

> Dan, I have been waiting for you to quiet yourself enough to hear Me speak to you. You think there is nothing new you can experience from me, but you are not right.
>
> There is much more that I have for you, things that are good. If you would but wait on me, spend time with me, I will begin to show you what I have for you.
>
> You say you want son-ship, but you have been cheating me of father-ship. It is like you are on your own and still complaining of distance. I'm still here, and I have not forsaken you.
>
> It hurts my heart when I hear you say you are far from me because you are not, you only think so. I forgive you for your ambivalence to my presence. I want you to feel good about our relationship not because it is the right thing to do but because you actually get some joy out of it.
>
> Find that place, and I will meet you there.
>
> God

How are you feeling right now? Did that prayer and response scare you at all? Make you uncomfortable? Did you say to yourself, "I'm not going to do that. I'm not going to allow myself to feel those things that I have stuffed over the years. I'm not going to be honest in my relationship with God"?

I'd invite you to try your best to leave those thoughts aside, read the book, then return if you have to and write the prayer and response. You might not be thanking me now, but you will be thanking me then.

Let's together pray the following prayer:

Prayer of Invitation

Father God, I invite Your Holy Spirit to come visit me, to teach me, to comfort me, and to draw me closer to You. I give You permission to move upon my heart, to perform surgery if necessary, so that my relationship with You will find the intimacy that You long for with me.

CHAPTER 1

WHY WAS I CREATED?

> For God so loved the world that he gave his one and only Son, that whoever believes in him shall not perish but have eternal life. For God did not send his Son into the world to condemn the world, but to save the world through him.
> —John 3:16–17

> After Jesus said this, he looked toward heaven and prayed: "Father, the time has come. Glorify your Son, that your Son may glorify you. For you granted him authority over all people that he might give eternal life to all those you have given him. Now this is eternal life: that they may know you, the only true God, and Jesus Christ, whom you have sent. I have brought you glory on
> — John 17:1–4

Why was I created? Isn't that the question for all eternity? Isn't that the question people much smarter than me have been grappling with since the dawn of time? How could I be so cheeky as to say I have the answer? I don't know, but I do.

Why was I created? Hmm, let's see. As a worship leader, someone who loves leading people into the presence of God, I could make a strong argument that I was created for worship, that is my destiny, and when I'm walking in my destiny, all else fades away.

I once was given the T-shirt, "Created to worship," so I could answer the "Why was I created?" question with, "To worship God." I could, but I won't.

Why was I created? Some have said to me that they were created for acts of service.

They were created to serve God through acts of service. That is their destiny, their intended purpose. They are driven to perform the "calling" they feel is on their lives. I could only pray that they stay healthy or that nothing interrupts that service because if they are not serving God, they are not living up to their intended purpose, why they were created.

> With every question, there is a "right answer" and a "more right answer."

Why was I created? Maybe it was to benefit mankind somehow, to leave my mark and disappear into eternity with some kind of lasting legacy. When they think of me, they will think of my legacy; this leaves just one question: who are they? You might say to me, numbers are not important. If I can affect just one life, I have lived my destiny, and I can die in peace.

All the above are great answers. I'm sure there are others. It's like a multiple choice test, though. With every question, there is a "right answer" and a "more right answer." On any test, if you check off the "right answer," you will get the question wrong. You must get the "more right answer" to pass the test.

So what is the "more right answer"?

Are you ready? Here goes…

Wait a sec. Let's go back to the Garden of Eden first. When God created man "in our image," in the image of the Trinity, he placed him in the garden. When I look at the Genesis account of Adam, I do not read anywhere that he worshipped God, where he walked around with his hands in the air, saying, "Hallelujah, thank you, God, for my life and all You do," or that he sat on a rock with a prayer book in deep meditation and reflection.

I also do not see Adam serving God, trying to make God happy somehow. He did not ask the question, "How am I doing, God?"

Nothing of what he did or said was based on performance. Also, there was no one else in the garden, so if it wasn't service to God but service to others that we are created for, then that argument falls flat pretty quickly.

What we do see Adam doing (I am all about original intention) is walking and talking with God. To finally answer the question, "Why was I created," the answer is for a *relationship with God*.

Out of that relationship comes worship and service. When you love someone and are in right relationship with them all you want to do is to love on them (worship), talk with them (prayer), tell others about them (evangelism), and make sure others know who they really are (discipleship).

> God's intent was fellowship… the reason we were created!

The reason I ended up there is by looking at the intention of God and what was broken when Adam sinned. Adam's service to God or to others was not affected by his sin of disobedience when he ate of the fruit of the tree. What was broken was relationship. Sin came between God and man.

God's intent was fellowship… the reason we were created! That intent was interrupted when Adam ate of the fruit, disobeying the very command of God not to eat of it. After Adam had sinned, God came looking for Adam. He said, "Adam, where are you?" God was pursuing relationship.

The devil's temptation was that Adam would become "like" God, but he ended up being distanced from God.

It was all about the fact of the relationship being broken, so it will come as no surprise then when I take you to the intention of the cross; it was not to just take away the sins of the world.

Taking away the sins of the world is far from the intention. The actual intention of the cross was to restore relationship between God and man. The cross was a means to "reconcile" man's relationship with God.

To reconcile means to bring two parties together who were once in relationship. That's what Jesus did at the cross; He brought sinful man and a holy God together by being the only sacrifice that could satisfy a holy God.

Man has tried throughout the centuries to bridge the gap between God and man, once trying to build a tower to the sky (see Babel) but mostly by trying to be holy enough so that God would somehow notice and allow one of them close.

> Those that try by their own righteousness to win
> God's favor are on a fruitless journey.

There's a fundamental flaw in that thinking. No one on earth could possibly be holy enough for God. Isaiah once wrote that all our righteousness (all the good things we say, do, are) are like filthy rags to God. The apostle Paul in his letter to the Romans says that no one is righteous, not even one.

Those that try by their own righteousness to win God's favor are on a fruitless journey. At the end of the road, it will all be for naught. It will be like climbing up this tall ladder only to find out when you reach the top, the ladder is leaning against the wrong building.

At the end of the day, it is not about man ascending to God (many examples, all failures) but rather God descending to man. In the great romance of God and man, God is the initiator, and His initiating cost Him a great deal: His only Son.

But when He (God) weighed the options, there was no price too high to pay for restored relationship with us humans. He missed us that much. Even when He was turning His back on His only Son who, on the cross, had taken on the sins of the world, God endured that agony for restored relationship.

So how'd we miss that? How'd we substitute activity in trying to impress God for resting in right relationship? I have learned the answer to this question as well! Read on.

When the devil, Satan, Lucifer, or whatever you want to call him (I've given him a few choice names!) was kicked out of heaven, he took with him one-third of the angels. He was also given authority over the earth as the "god of this earth" as the apostle Paul would say.

Being "people of the earth," we are born under his authority. If we die under his authority, we are sent to hell, a place reserved for the devil and those under his authority.

Only when we choose a greater authority will we be able to break free from Satan's authority, and the only authority greater is Jesus, Lord of lords and King of kings.

When people say they are born again, what they are actually saying is that they are being transferred from one kingdom (the kingdom of darkness) to another kingdom (the kingdom of God's son). They are simply placing themselves under a new and greater authority and, in so doing, coming back into relationship with God the Father.

> At that very point Adam turned away from God
> and toward the tree, and this was the beginning
> of the relationship being broken.

That's why the devil tempted Adam to break relationship between Adam and God. To break relationship between two people, all you have to do is sow a little mistrust. When the devil said, "Did God say..." he was placing mistrust in Adam's mind that *maybe* God wasn't telling him the whole truth.

At that very point, Adam turned away from God and toward the tree, and this was the beginning of the relationship being broken.

Let's take this a step further. Once someone is transferred from the devil's kingdom to God's kingdom, the devil's work changes slightly because he has lost this soul to God, but his intention never changes. His goal, his motivation, his driving force is to break relationship between God and man.

Why in the world do you think we are still tempted *after* we get saved? I remember this one man thinking that once he found the woman of his dreams, he would never look at another woman. No other woman would ever be attractive to him. Boy, was he wrong!

> If the devil can get you thinking that relationship
> with God is all about holiness, he has you in the
> palm of his hand.

Once a person is saved, the devil knows he/she is gone. However, he also knows he can render them powerless by doing whatever he can to disturb the relationship. Temptation is part of his activity, along with stress, division, insecurity, backbiting—the list goes on. If the devil can get you focused on anything *but* your relationship with God, he wins—well, kind of. He cannot win you back, but he can make you ineffective.

If the devil can get you thinking that relationship with God is all about holiness, he has you in the palm of his hand. You will stay focused on what you do and not *who you are*, a child of God. For the record, I am not against holiness. What I am against is someone thinking it somehow draws God's attention.

Holiness is for *our* good, not God's. Holiness keeps us from those things that destroy and devastate lives. Holiness is better translated as "wholeness."

After all, our "holiness" comes from God and not from our own efforts. In receiving God's holiness through His Son, Jesus, we can no longer brag about our own righteousness. It's when we give up that pursuit of holiness that we actually can walk in holiness, God's holiness.

When you sin, instead of seeing it as a black mark next to your name in God's Book of Life, see it, rather, as breaking or, at the very least/most, distancing relationship between you and the Heavenly Father.

And when we confess our sins in that light, God forgives our sins and cleanses us from all unrighteousness, and the way is made clear once again for pure relationship.

> Put all of life through the filter of relationship
> with God and see how things change.

We will never live a sinless life so forget about trying. Actually one guy tried to tell me he was without sin, but in telling me, he was sinning, so if we will never live a sinless life (I know this question is on your mind), why try? Why try? Because it is *not about* our sin, it is about relationship with God.

Put all of life through the filter of relationship with God and see how things change. See how you change. And see how the people around you will be more drawn to you than before because the pressure of having to be good (or holy) is gone. It has been replaced with a relationship of rest. We never have to impress God or win his affections. He loves us just as we are. That is so freeing.

Remember, it is all about relationship. *We were created for relationship with God.* Nothing short of that will do or satisfy. Pursue it (relationship with God) with all your heart, soul, mind, and strength. That is what life is all about.

Discussion:

1. What was I created for?
2. What caused distance between man and God?
3. What has man done to bridge that distance?
4. Has it worked?
5. Who/what bridged the distance?
6. Why was the distance bridged?
7. What should be my response?

Action Plan:

Today I…

(This is what I learned.)

And I…

(This is how I will apply what I learned.)

CHAPTER 2

THE FATHER IS

I was born and raised in the Okanagan valley in a place called Kelowna, British Columbia. I have often said that is where God started creating the world because of its beauty and Edenic nature. Much fruit is grown in that valley, everything from apples, peaches, plums to cherries, pears, and apricots.

> If I went to the God-tree, what kind of fruit would I pick?

One thing you find out fairly quickly is that if you go to an apple tree and pick its fruit, you will without question pick an apple (or as one person said in a concert of mine once, "Unless you pick two, then it would be a pear." You'll get that one in about five minutes!).

But with that thought in mind, it begs the question, "If I went to the God-tree, what kind of fruit would I pick?"

One night, I was invited over for supper to a young couple's house. I was thinking about this very question, and then with a sureness I knew was from God, the fruit of the Spirit from Galatians 5 came to my mind.

I was hardly in the door when I asked for a Bible. Seeing a guitar in the corner, I asked permission as well and wrote the following song:

> The Father Is…
> (C) 1994 Dan Thiessen
>
> Chorus:
>
> The Father is love,
> The Father is joy,
> The Father is patient
> The Father is peace,
> The Father is good,
> The Father is gentleness and faith
> The Father is meek,
> To all who would seek,
> The Father is temperance
> He loves me so much,
> And against such,
> There is no law

Why not take the next few minutes and go through these descriptions of God? A question I often ask when someone tries to tell me something or teach me a concept is, "What does that look like?"

Below, and next to each word, write what those words look like in relation to God the Father.

> But the fruit of the Spirit is love, joy, peace, patience, kindness, goodness, faithfulness, gentleness and self-control. Against such things there is no law. (Gal. 5:22–23)

Love –

Joy –

Peace –

Patience –

Kindness –

Goodness –

Faithfulness –

Gentleness –

Self-Control –

Probably the most quoted wedding scripture ever is 1 Corinthians 13. Why? Well, it is because that is the model of what love is supposed to look like. Everyone knows the phrase, "God is love," but not everyone knows how this kind of love is put into action.

What if God was your prospective spouse and you found these words described Him? Would that draw you to Him or away from Him?

> Love is patient, love is kind. It does not envy, it does not boast, it is not proud. It is not rude, it is not self-seeking, it is not easily angered, keeps no record of wrongs. Love does not delight in evil but rejoices with the truth. It always protects, always trusts, always hopes, always perseveres. Love never fails. (1 Cor. 13:4–8)

SEEING GOD

Patient –

Kind –

Does not envy –

Does not boast –

Not proud –

Not rude –

Not self-seeking –

Not easily angered –

Does not keep a record of wrongs –

Does not delight in evil –

Rejoices in truth –

Always protects –

Always trusts –

Always hopes –

Always perseveres –

Never fails -

    Again, "who we perceive God to be determines how close we get to Him." I ask the question though it might seem incredibly redundant. If the world (or you) saw God as these two passages of Scripture, would they be drawn to Him or away from him?

Back in the year 2000, my family had a reunion. I come from a large family of ten children. The reunion was held on a Saturday out in the Vancouver area. On the Sunday morning, I had arranged to speak at a church in Surrey.

Most of my siblings were in attendance (no pressure!). I was the ninth of the ten children, so much life had happened to my family before I came along. Part of that "much life" came as a result of how the church treated my family.

> If that's who God is, you can have Him. I don't want relationship with a God like that.

My brothers especially grew up hating the church and, by extension, hated God (well, maybe not hated but didn't like Him very much and certainly didn't want to be in relationship with Him—kind of the old, "If that's who God is, you can have Him. I don't want relationship with a God like that" attitude).

I find it so interesting that most of people's wrong perceptions of God come from the body of Christ. That is to our shame. Whether through experience or wrong teaching, we pick up these perceptions along the way.

Add those wrong perceptions to our own insecurities and there's no way we could ever have a good relationship with God (or want to).

I say all this to say that following my sermon and singing a few songs, one of my brothers said to me a statement that will last me a lifetime. He said, "If this is who God really is, I can serve that kind of God."

Wow, I thought, did the church ever miss it!

Sad to say, many churches/ministries talk "about" God out of study and research but not out of personal experience. The word "to know" in the Bible when it refers to knowing God is an experiential word meaning "to come into living, breathing contact with someone."

> So do you know God? Do you know His tendencies, the way He would react in certain situations?

Imagine hearing about someone through friends enough to feel like you know them. They are a well-known personality, so you go on the Internet or to the library (does anyone read books anymore?) and research this person. You feel you know this person. Then comes the day when you have an opportunity to meet them.

You are in the same room where you can hear their voice, you can smell them, see how they move physically. You can look into their eyes and see their soul. Before you knew about them, now you are meeting them and then knowing them with all their idiosyncrasies. They are nowhere close to who you thought them to be.

So do you know God? Do you know His tendencies, the way He would react in certain situations? Do you know what flavor ice cream He would order at Ben & Jerry's? It is all about knowing and being known. King David, when referred to in the book of Acts, was called, "a man after God's own heart." To me, this is the highest of all compliments. Why was he a man after God's own heart? Is it because he knew more than anybody about God? Was he researching while he tended his father's sheep? Or did he allow God to pursue him to know and be known?

Read Psalm 139:1–6, 23–24 (MSG):

> God, investigate my life; get all the facts firsthand. I'm an open book to you; even from a distance, you know what I'm thinking. You know when I leave and when I get back; I'm never out of your sight. You know everything I'm going to say before I start the first sentence. I look behind me and you're there, then up ahead and you're there, too— your reassuring presence, coming and going. This is too much, too wonderful—I can't take it all in!

> Investigate my life, O God, find out everything about me; Cross-examine and test me, get a clear picture of what I'm about; See for yourself whether I've done anything wrong—then guide me on the road to eternal life.

These are the words of a man who knew God and was known by Him. He didn't just know *about* God, he *knew* God!

Wouldn't it be better for people to experience God firsthand than through someone else? The Samaritan woman at the well, after her one on one encounter with Jesus, ran back to her community and didn't set up a soapbox to tell people about her experience. She simply said, "Come and see," then brought them out to meet Jesus.

> One big part that we often overlook is God's desire to have relationship with us.

Methinks if we spent more time inviting people to meet Jesus and less time inviting people to church or church events, more people would come to church. Does this make sense (it does in my head!)?

I am not belittling church or church events in the least. I just think sometimes we put the cart before the horse. What is the old axiom, "Form follows function"?

One big part that we often overlook is God's desire to have relationship with us. He pursues us. His heart is toward us. Check out these words in Hosea 6:6 (NLT):

> I want you to show love, not offer sacrifices. I want you to know me more than I want burnt offerings.

The Scripture that says, "No one comes to the Father except the Father draws him" says to me that when we feel the tug of the Spirit of God, that is the Father saying, "Hey you, I want relationship with you. Are you up for it?"

For those raised in church always knowing "about" God, you know that the way of God is the right way. Maybe you don't know God personally, but you know God is the right way to go.

When I was a child, I was leading my friends to the Lord with the sinner's prayer, but I knew in my heart I did not know Him like He could be known. In my childhood, I lived one of those "good" lives (except when I got caught stealing milk money, a story for another day), so much so that my church wanted to baptize me.

But I knew in my heart of hearts that I wasn't quite there yet. When I made a commitment to follow Jesus wholeheartedly when I was sixteen or seventeen, I jumped in with both feet. I was baptized in a lake and called to ministry all that same year. I have been in some sort of ministry ever since.

> God came to me around that time and revealed Himself as a Father.

God has been progressively revealing His character and nature to me throughout my life. There are a number of touchstones that I reflect upon.

The first touchstone is when my mother left my father I was ten years old. I remained with my father. This was the same year my next oldest brother (who was a kind of replacement dad for me as I had virtually no relationship with my dad) left for the military. I felt so completely alone and abandoned.

God came to me around that time and revealed Himself as a Father. He said to me that He would be my father. He would raise me and teach me the way I should go. His presence would be real in my life, and He would never leave me or forsake me.

My dad would sometimes complain that I was too polite, too nice to people and too accommodating. He knew he hadn't taught me to respect my elders, open doors for people, stand when people enter the room, never hit a girl (that one was tough!) and more. I learned those from my Heavenly Father.

A second touchstone was around the same time we had taken in a boarder, someone to rent a bedroom in our house. His name was Ray Watson, and he was of African American descent.

As a child, I saw no difference in our skin color and developed quite an affinity for him. Because I was being fathered by my Heavenly Father, I was quick to defend if Ray was called a name or whatever.

This is how God thinks, it's in his heart, and I learned it from the source. It doesn't matter about color, race, religion, gender, or any earthly thing that might separate us.

We are all equal in God's sight, and not only equal but precious. And by being precious, we are worthy of His love. And by being worthy of His love, we become the objects of His affection.

How cool is that!

Discussion:

1. What fruit comes from the God tree?
2. What does God's love look like?
3. What does your love for God look like?
4. What would people say God is like when watching you?
5. If God were to have a favorite ice cream flavor, what would it be and why?
6. What does it mean to be "after God's heart" like the book of Acts says about King David?

Action Plan:

Today I…

(This is what I learned.)

And I…

(This is how I will apply what I learned.)

Chapter 3

Jesus and the Father

> "If you really knew me, you would know my Father as well.
> From now on, you do know him and have seen him."
> Philip said, "Lord, show us the Father and
> that will be enough for us."
> Jesus answered: "Don't you know me, Philip, even after I have
> been among you such a long time? Anyone who has seen me
> has seen the Father. How can you say, 'Show us the Father'?
> Don't you believe that I am in the Father, and that the Father
> is in me? The words I say to you are not just my own. Rather,
> it is the Father, living in me, who is doing his work."
> —John 14:7–10

When Jesus was on the earth, He was the expression of God's tangible love for us, so it makes sense to me that if we looked at how Jesus responded to things, we would find out a whole lot about what His Father is like. After all, Jesus used phrases like, "If you have seen Me you have seen the Father" and "I do only what I see the Father doing."

There is one story that, in my mind, epitomizes the character and nature of God revealed through His Son. That is the story of the woman caught in adultery in John 8.

To set this up, we must remember that Jesus has been teaching and performing miracles. His authority is evident, so much so the reigning spiritual authorities (Scribes and Pharisees) are getting threatened. They set out to discredit Him. If they can reduce His profile and reputation, they can diffuse His influence, and they will once again rule the people who know *about* God but never know Him.

To provoke a response from Jesus, one of their own entices a woman to sleep with him so that they can come, catch her "in the very act," and bring her to Jesus with expectations of trapping Him.

They hope to ask Him a hard question pertaining to a woman caught in adultery and simply wait. Somewhere along the way their plan goes awry.

> "Teacher, this woman has been caught in adultery, in the very act. Moses, in the Law, says she must be stoned. What do you say?"

The woman is dragged and thrown before Jesus, who had been teaching in the synagogue area (so there would be lots of people as witnesses). He greets them with His eyes, and they greet Him with a question, "Teacher, this woman has been caught in adultery, in the very act. Moses, in the Law, says she must be stoned. What do you say?"

With the wisdom and poise of eternity, Jesus does not respond verbally but rather kneels and begins to write on the ground the Ten Commandments (of which the Scribes and Pharisees are abundantly acquainted). He lifts up His head and says to His beckoning crowd, "Let him that has no sin cast the first stone." Then he waits.

Jesus knows the Law better than the Scribes and Pharisees. After all, His Father transcribed the first set. Jesus knows the woman is guilty and according to the Law should be put to death. No one is throwing a stone at the woman, but also no one is leaving. Jesus returns to His knee and begins to write again.

This time Jesus begins to write the names of the Scribes and Pharisees and under each name begins to write *their* sins. I think this would be a tad embarrassing for the Scribes and Pharisees.

Subsequently, they begin to dissipate, from the oldest to the youngest, till there were none of the accusers left. Only the woman stood before Jesus.

Jesus speaks to her. He asks, "Where are your accusers?"

"They are gone" she replies, still nervously waiting for the Teacher to pick up a stone and strike her. He speaks, but what she hears is not what she was expecting. What He says takes her breath away: "Neither do I condemn you. Go and sin no more."

> If God the Father were there He would have said the same thing as Jesus because Jesus never said or did anything without observing His Father first.

Jesus's response reminds me of a phrase from possibly one of the observers in the crowd to let mercy triumph over judgment (James). This is God's heart. This is who we are to know God to be. If God the Father were there He would have said the same thing as Jesus because Jesus never said or did anything without observing His Father first.

The most popular verse in the Bible no doubt is John 3:16. Most Christians can quote at least some semblance of the verse, "For God so loved the world…" You know the rest. However, not as many can quote the next verse, verse 17.

To paraphrase, "For God didn't send His son into the world to condemn the world but that the world through Him would be saved."

Jesus didn't come pointing a finger at us but rather beckoning us with His hand, calling us *to* the Father not *away* from Him.

Who Was Jesus Mad At?

One way to really get to know someone is to see what makes them angry, to see what gets under their skin, irritates them, invokes a reaction. We have a couple of examples of Jesus "losing it," and we would do well to learn from him. The examples are when Jesus twice got angry at the sellers and traders in the Temple.

Righteous Anger in His Father's House

We are taught from childhood that anger is wrong and that we are to rid our character of that dastardly emotion. I'm not sure where we got this idea, but it wasn't from modeling Jesus. He got *really* angry—twice! I'm not saying that all anger is appropriate, so what made Jesus's anger right?

Let's examine these flare-ups as one. He is walking to the Temple, and he hears the sellers and traders bartering and exchanging money on the holy grounds of the Temple. He rushes in, begins tipping tables, and after grabbing some sort of whip, starts to scare everyone out of there.

See the verses below and examine if you can identify what separates this anger from the anger we are not supposed to show.

> Jesus entered the temple area and drove out all who were buying and selling there. He overturned the tables of the money changers and the benches of those selling doves. "It is written," he said to them," 'My house will be called a house of prayer, but you are making it a 'den of robbers. (Matt. 21:12–13)

The key words in this expression of anger (anyone want to take a guess?) are "My Father's house." Anger that is in defense of someone else is, more often than not, appropriate anger. Where we dip into the inappropriate anger zone is where our anger is in defense of ourselves.

I once attended a "Spring of Life" pro-life/pro-choice demonstration in Buffalo, New York. There were thousands of people lining this one street. On one side of the street, there were the pro-choice advocates, and on the other side of the street, there were the pro-lifers. Each group was just as passionate about their cause, each one showing anger in defense of someone or something.

> It is God's nature to defend the defenseless, the fatherless and the widows in their affliction, the army that has three hundred against the enemies' three hundred thousand.

I was there to defend the rights of those who *didn't* have a voice, the unborn. I have no doubt where Jesus would have been if He were physically present on the earth.

It is God's nature to defend the defenseless, the fatherless, and the widows in their affliction, the army that has three hundred against the enemies' three hundred thousand. It is consistent throughout Scripture.

Here is the song I was at the rally to sing. It is from Psalm 139, and it is uniquely written from the perspective of the unborn child.

I Am a Heartbeat
Dan Thiessen © 1991

CHORUS:
I am a heartbeat and I am alive
I've just started living, I'm not ready to die
I have a voice but you can't hear my cry
I am a heartbeat and I am alive

VERSE ONE:
I have been fearfully, wonderfully made
Before I was formed I was known
My God has possessed me before my days
And covered me while in the womb
His eyes did see me, yet being unformed
In His book all my parts written down
How precious are all of Thy thoughts unto me
O God, and how great is the sum

VERSE TWO:

O Lord, You have searched me and I am known,
You see when I sit or I rise
You compass my path and my lying down,
There's nowhere to hide from Your eyes

Where shall I go from Thy Spirit, O Lord?
And where shall I hide from Your face?
If I ascend up or I sleep down below,
Your hand shall establish my ways

BRIDGE:
God in His wisdom, allows the decision
Am I going to die, am I going to die?
I beg for your mercy, as I pray that you'll see
The life you allow is alive even now

At the Devil

> Jesus turned and said to Peter, "Get behind me, Satan! You are a stumbling block to me; you do not have in mind the things of God, but the things of men." (Matt. 16:23)

Was Jesus mad at Peter in this verse (even if He did say a stupid thing)? Not all, because Jesus knew where that stupid statement came from, the devil himself. If the devil could convince Jesus through Peter to *not* die, then the whole plan of reconciliation would fall flat on its face, and the devil would maintain his authority.

Jesus was quite aware of that plan. Remember the temptation in the wilderness. Jesus knew better than to take out His anger on Peter but rather on the devil. We would do well to learn something here.

> Focusing our anger on the appropriate subjects is taking on more and more of God's character.

The apostle Paul teaches us that our warfare is not against flesh and blood (people we can see), but rather our warfare is in a spiritual realm (spirits we cannot see). Lord, give us wisdom to know the difference.

Here's a thought. Next time there is an argument between you and your spouse or between friends or, God forbid, a church split, instead of blowing a fuse at the enemy you can see, why not take a shot at the enemy you cannot see, the devil. After all, his purpose is to divide and conquer, right?

Focusing our anger on the appropriate subjects is taking on more and more of God's character. Let's be mad at what God is mad at.

At the Pharisees (in their Pride and Spiritual Blindness)

Read the following Scriptures and see if you can make the same connection I did.

> There are six things the LORD hates, seven that are detestable to him: haughty eyes, a lying tongue, hands that shed innocent blood, a heart that devises wicked schemes, feet that are quick to rush into evil, a false witness who pours out lies and a man who stirs up dissension among brothers. (Prov. 6:16–19)

> "Woe to you, teachers of the law and Pharisees, you hypocrites! You give a tenth of your spices—mint, dill and cumin. But you have neglected the more important matters of the law—justice, mercy and faithfulness. You should have practiced the latter, without neglecting the former.

You blind guides! You strain out a gnat but swallow a camel.

"Woe to you, teachers of the law and Pharisees, you hypocrites! You clean the outside of the cup and dish, but inside they are full of greed and self-indulgence. Blind Pharisee! First clean the inside of the cup and dish, and then the outside also will be clean.

"Woe to you, teachers of the law and Pharisees, you hypocrites! You are like whitewashed tombs, which look beautiful on the outside but on the inside are full of dead men's bones and everything unclean. In the same way, on the outside you appear to people as righteous but on the inside you are full of hypocrisy and wickedness.

"Woe to you, teachers of the law and Pharisees, you hypocrites! You build tombs for the prophets and decorate the graves of the righteous. And you say, 'If we had lived in the days of our forefathers, we would not have taken part with them in shedding the blood of the prophets.' So you testify against yourselves that you are the descendants of those who murdered the prophets. Fill up, then, the measure of the sin of your forefathers!

"You snakes! You brood of vipers! How will you escape being condemned to hell? Therefore I am sending you prophets and wise men and teachers. Some of them you will kill and crucify; others you will flog in your synagogues and pursue from town to town. And so upon you will come all the righteous blood that has been shed on earth, from the blood of righteous Abel to the blood of Zechariah son of Berekiah, whom you murdered between the temple and the altar.

I tell you the truth, all this will come upon this generation.

"O Jerusalem, Jerusalem, you who kill the prophets and stone those sent to you, how often I have longed to gather your children together, as a hen gathers her chicks under her wings, but you were not willing. Look, your house is left to you desolate." (Matt. 23:23–38)

In these verses from the Proverbs, we see a list of things God hates, with pride making its way to the top of the list. I'd like to take this list a step further and see how the Scribes and Pharisees took on each characteristic that God hates. No wonder Jesus gets so upset in the Matthew scripture that follows.

1. Haughty eyes (pride)
2. Lying tongue
3. Hands that shed innocent blood
4. A heart that devises wicked schemes
5. Feet that are quick to run into evil
6. A false witness that pours out lies
7. A man who stirs up dissension among brothers

Discussion:

1. When Jesus said, "If you have seen me you have seen the Father," what did he mean?
2. What does it mean to know about God but not know Him like Jesus said about the Pharisees?
3. If you had sinned like the woman caught in adultery, what response would you expect from God?
4. What fuels appropriate anger?
5. What kinds of things are okay to be angry about?
6. What does God hate the most?

Action Plan:

Today I...

(This is what I learned.)

And I...

(This is how I will apply what I learned.)

CHAPTER 4

Hearing God's Voice

> My sheep listen to my voice;
> I know them, and they follow me.
> —John 10:27

God, the Devil, or Bad Pizza

All of us hear voices or have thoughts inside our head. Some hear more than others! I would like to talk about three of those voices. I call this section "God, the devil or bad pizza" because not everything we hear is either God or the devil.

If we begin thinking that way, that there are only two sources to the voices in our head, then we set ourselves up for a lot of inner anguish trying to discern what is from whom.

> If what you are hearing makes you feel bad about yourself, it is from the devil. If the voice makes you feel bad about what you have done, it is from God.

I mentioned from the beginning that I like to simplify things. This next statement might be the simplest of all: If what you are hearing makes you feel bad about yourself, it is from the devil. If the voice makes you feel bad about what you have done, it is from God.

Let me explain by giving you one of the names/descriptions of the devil, it is the "accuser of the brethren" (and sistern!). What that tells me is that he is the prosecuting attorney, and Jesus is the defense attorney. The prosecution brings all sorts of accusations against us (hoping one will stick!).

The truth of the matter, sadly, is that there is truth in what he is saying.

There is an interesting verse in 1 John 2:1–2:

> My dear children, I write this to you so that you will not sin. But if anybody does sin, we have one who speaks to the Father in our defense—Jesus Christ, the Righteous One. He is the atoning sacrifice for our sins, and not only for ours but also for the sins of the whole world.

"One who speaks to the Father in our defense"—sounds like a defense attorney to me. One who has never lost a case, I might add.

> God, however, deals with what we have done and
> builds up who we are.

As an accuser/prosecuting attorney, the devil would rather attack the person than the activity. This sounds like, "You idiot, you are so stupid. How could you ever have done something like that? I told you, you would, and you did. You are such a failure." (Sound familiar?)

God, however, deals with what we have done and builds up who we are. His words are more like, "You know you did wrong there. Confess it so you can be forgiven. I believe in you. You don't have to be a slave to that stuff anymore. You are worth more than that stuff. Turn your back on that activity. Walk away [repent] and chart a new course. I will help you all along the way."

As I understand it, there is a difference between guilt and conviction. Guilt produces condemnation, and is weighty and often unbearable. It leads us away from God and not toward Him.

Conviction, however, produces confession and repentance, which leads to forgiveness and freedom. This process will lead us back to the Father, not away from Him.

I find it very interesting that after the apostle Paul wrote the well-known chapter (Romans 7) about doing things he knows are wrong and not doing things he knows are right, he introduces us to one of the great verses in the Bible in Romans 8:1 (NIV):

> Therefore, there is now no condemnation for
> those who are in Christ Jesus.

Condemnation, therefore, cannot be from God. If you are feeling condemned, this *cannot* be from God. Address it as such. Command it to leave in the name of Jesus. Tell the devil you know it's him and won't be fooled anymore.

What Does God's Voice Sound Like?

When someone calls us on the telephone, those who call us the most have the most recognizable voices. When I'm calling someone I know, I will often disguise my voice to throw them off a bit.

However, some of my friends know me so well they can hear through the fake accent and call my bluff! Why? Because they know me!

So what does God's voice sound like? Consider the following:

If we filter God's voice through His character and nature, then any words that are

- condemning,
- judgmental,
- attacking our person (who we are),
- tempting,
- controlling,
- intimidating,
- coercing,

- manipulating, or
- lies

are not from Him. They can't be. They would be inconsistent with His character and nature. Imagine, if you will, an acquaintance coming to you with words they thought they heard your best friend say, negative, nasty words.

> Wouldn't the church in general be so much better off if they knew God more than if they knew more about God?

But you know your friend. You know they would never talk that way or even use those words. What do you say to your acquaintance? You likely say, "My friend would never speak like that. I choose not to believe those words because they are so out of character with who I know my friend to be."

Wouldn't the church in general be so much better off if they knew God more than if they knew more about God?

God's Holy Spirit (His Voice)

God's voice is often communicated to us through the Holy Spirit. Let's see what name(s) the Holy Spirit is given. Let's see, hmm, His names means "comforter, guide, edifier, exhorter."

They don't sound very negative, do they? The purpose of the Holy Spirit is to draw us "to" the Father, not "away" from the Father.

When the Holy Spirit speaks, He will

- convict us of sin,
- draw us to the Father,
- edify,
- exhort,
- comfort,

- build us up (does not tear down), and
- draw attention to Jesus, never to Himself.

Back to the section title, "God, the Devil, or Bad Pizza." Sometimes we hear things in our head that are simply wishful thinking, or hopes and dreams, or, on the negative side, anger, resentment or bitterness.

These words are neither from God nor from the devil, just like every event in our lives cannot be attributed to either God or the devil.

As Joni Eareckson once said about that terrible diving accident that left her paralyzed from the neck down, "Neither God nor the devil caused the accident. But both God AND the devil showed interest in it. God showed interest because He wanted to comfort me through the upcoming journey and the devil, because He wanted me to curse God."

Not everything we hear in our head is from God or the devil. Maybe it could be the bad pizza making you think crazy, who knows. Well, actually, you can know, if you choose to know God's voice.

> I would much rather encourage you to get to
> know God, His voice, His character and nature.

I have never been one for studying the devil much. I was told once upon a time that tellers at a certain bank while in training would never handle counterfeit money. The intention was that once they had exclusively dealt with the "real thing," when anything different came along, they would readily identify it.

I would much rather encourage you to get to know God, His voice, His character and nature. If you spend all this quality time getting to know Him, you will readily recognize a voice or a thought that is contrary to God's character and nature. Make sense?

Discussion:

1. What does God's voice sound like?
2. What is the difference between conviction and guilt/condemnation?
3. Who do you blame when something bad happens?
4. Whose voice do you more easily recognize: God, the devil, or bad pizza?

Action Plan:

Today I…

(This is what I learned.)

And I…

(This is how I will apply what I learned.)

Chapter 5

City of Refuge

> God is our refuge and our strength,
> a very present help in trouble.
>
> —Psalm 46:1

We are all cave dwellers to some degree. What is the reason? It's not safe out there!

For a lot of people, God is not safe, not because of who God really is but more for who these people have been told God is.

Cities of Refuge

Premise

In a nutshell, when God was setting up what life would look like in the "Promised Land," he established cities of refuge. These cities of refuge were for those who had accidentally or in self-defense killed someone.

Because the law at the time said "An eye for an eye and a tooth for a tooth," these people were now in danger for their lives, especially because of the secondary part to the above law.

In those days, when someone in your family was killed by accident or otherwise, you could appoint an "avenger of blood" to pay retribution (kill the offender).

For the accused's protection, God set up these cities of refuge for the innocent to run into and be safe. As long as they lived inside those city walls, they were protected.

> Then the LORD said to Moses: "Speak to the Israelites and say to them: 'When you cross the Jordan into Canaan, select some towns to be your cities of refuge, to which a person who has killed someone accidentally may flee. They will be places of refuge from the avenger, so that a person accused of murder may not die before he stands trial before the assembly. These six towns you give will be your cities of refuge. Give three on this side of the Jordan and three in Canaan as cities of refuge. These six towns will be a place of refuge for Israelites, aliens and any other people living among them, so that anyone who has killed another accidentally can flee there." (Num. 35:9–15)

In the Old Testament, we see cities of refuge that were places of safety. Each city had a name that carried with it an appropriate translation to convey the nature and character of God. The names are found in Joshua 20:7–9:

1. Kedesh
   - "sacred, holy place, cleansing"
   - When Isaiah was ushered into the presence of God, he heard only one song:

   Holy, holy, holy is the Lord of hosts. (Isa. 6:3)

   One of the names of God is Jehovah Makedesh, "I AM the LORD your holiness."

-We can run into His holiness because we are now, "the righteousness of God in Him (Christ)" (2 Cor. 5:21).

2. Shechem
   - "shoulder, burden bearer"

   Cast your care upon Him for He careth for you. (1 Pet. 5:7)

   Come unto me all ye that are heavy laden, and I will give you rest. (Matt. 11:28)

3. Hebron
   -"fellowship"

   That which we have seen and heard declare we unto you, that ye also may have fellowship with us; and truly our fellowship is with the Father, and with His Son, Jesus Christ. (1 John 1:3)

   Behold, I stand at the door and knock; if any man hear My voice, and open the door, I will come in to him, and will sup with him, and he with me. (Rev. 3:20)

4. Bezer
   - "stronghold, fortress"

   The Lord thy God in the midst of thee is mighty. (Zeph. 3:17)

   O Lord, my strength, and my fortress. (Jer. 16:19)

   A Mighty Fortress is Our God. (Martin Luther.)

5. Ramoth
   - "exalted, lifted up"

Humble yourselves in the sight of the Lord, and He shall lift you up. (James 4:10)

For promotion cometh neither from the east, nor from the west, nor from the south. But God is the judge; He putteth down one, and setteth up another. (Ps. 75:6–7)

6. Golan
   - "separation, apart from temptation"

Wherefore, come out from among them, and be ye separate, saith the Lord, and touch not the unclean thing; and I will receive you, And will be a father unto you, and ye shall be my sons and daughters, saith the Lord Almighty. (2 Cor.6:17–18)

God calls us to Himself as a refuge.

My Beloved spoke and He said to me, Rise up, my love, my fair one, and come away. (Song of Sol. 2:10)

We might have a strong consolation, who have fled for refuge to lay hold upon the hope set before us. (Heb.6:18)

Can you now see that God set up these cities of refuge as a picture of Himself? Is He your city of refuge? When you sin, when you stumble and fall, do you run toward Him or away from Him? When my son was of school age, he was having a difficult time at school, being bullied and the like.

One day he came running home from school. I asked him why, of all the places he could run to, he would run home. His reply went deep into my spirit, "'Cause that's where I'm safe, Dad."

So what about you? When you are bullied and the like from life, can you see God as a city of refuge? You know you are safe there! I can say from personal experience that God indeed is my safe place, my city of refuge.

When I have fought accusation, attack, condemnation, and judgment, I realized I have a choice to run toward God or away from Him. Remember Richard Gere's character in *An Officer and a Gentleman*? He was trying his best to become a marine, but his past kept trying to be part of his present.

In one critical scene, he fights with his commanding officer and is expelled from the marines. There he is, this life-toughened man lying on the ground, crying, saying one of the most powerful lines of all time, "But I've got nowhere to go!"

> There is no other safe place. There is no other city of refuge.

The apostle Peter was declaring to Jesus as his teachings were getting more and more demanding that more and more followers were leaving. This prompted Jesus to ask Peter the hard question, "Will you also leave?"

Peter's answer was the precursor to the line in *An Officer and a Gentleman*, "But where am I to go? You are the way to eternal life."

In my life, I am often confronted with that decision, will I leave Him also? But because of my life experience with God and knowledge of His nature and character, I don't want to go anywhere else. There is no other safe place. There is no other city of refuge.

City of Refuge
Dan Thiessen © 1995

<u>Chorus:</u>
You are my City of Refuge
A place that I can run to
God, you are my shelter from the storm
You are my City of Refuge
A place that I can run to
God, I feel so safe within Your arms

<u>Verse:</u>
Here I stand, O Lord, in need of mercy
Guilty of the things I shouldn't do
Voices all around,
And yet Your grace abounds
You've given me a safe place I can run to

So again, it all comes down to how you view God. In the following chapters, we will take a look at how our wrong views of God have affected our worship, our prayer, our evangelism, and our fellowship.

Discussion:

1. What does the word *safe* mean to you?
2. When you fail/sin, are you more likely to run *to* God or run *away* from Him?
3. Are you "safe"? What does that look like?
4. How do you react to the phrase "You (God) love me as I am not as I was or hope to be"?

Action Plan:

Today I…

(This is what I learned)

And I…

(This is how I will apply what I learned)

CHAPTER 6

WORSHIP

How Does My View of God Affect My Worship?

As we take a look at how your view of God affects your worship, take a piece of paper and draw a line down the middle of it. On the one column put at the top "Wrong view," and on the second column put "Result."

Just to be sure we are going the same direction here, when I say worship, I mean the expressive adoration of all that God is and has done for you. Some people see worship as your daily life, living a life of worship. That is not the context for this discussion.

What I would like you to take a look at is when you go to church or play a worship CD, what is going on in your heart when the "music" part of worship begins. I know you are likely thinking about God. I am curious about what kinds of thoughts are flowing through your mind.

Are they positive or negative thoughts? Are you endearing or withdrawing? Loving or ambivalent? Someone once said that the opposite of love is not hate but apathy. Are your feelings connecting with God? If yes, you are heading the right direction. If not, why not?

At church, for some, worship is what stands in the way of them hearing the sermon. They can't wait for that part of the service (the singing part) to be over so they can get to the *real* reason they are there, to hear from the Word of God. I have found there are two schools of thought with regard to worship services as we know them.

One school says that the preaching of the Word is the climax of the service, the focal point if you will. The other school of thought is that the singing worship portion of a service is the climax, the focal point.

These viewpoints can sometimes be at odds with each other, causing tension between pastor and worship leader.

> If you have a wrong view of God, it will affect
> your drawing close to Him in singing worship.

Whatever school of thought is yours, if your focus on Sunday morning is *not* connecting with God, then you've missed it.

That would be a clear indicator that your relationship with God is failing. If you are focused entirely on information and not transformation, you are missing it.

Imagine being invited to someone's house with just you and them there and not talking with them. You move about the house, admiring artifacts and pictures, but never address your host, or if you do, it is in relation to something you are looking at. At some point, your host might wonder why you came in the first place.

If you have a wrong view of God, it will affect your drawing close to Him in singing worship. If you are angry with Him, you will not with reckless abandon run toward Him and cry out, "Abba Father." Your worship will be distant and obligatory. You will not be loving on God with all your heart, soul, mind, and strength.

The same would be true if you saw God as the "distant Almighty" who was not that interested in you personally but generally cared for the goings on of the world. Your worship would not be responsive or reflective but rather cold and filled with form.

Bette Midler once sang a song called "From a Distance." For some, that is their view of God, that God is way up there and they are way down here.

As long as they don't do anything too dramatic, life will go on, and God will not get too involved with their lives. For them, that would be a good thing.

> It is amazing when someone focuses so hard on *not* doing things wrong that they are more prone to do things wrong.

I was raised in a Mennonite Brethren culture and my perception of God as a child was that He was so big, so awesome, so mighty (so scary) that how could He be personal?

I thought God might be like the principal I had in elementary school, who walked and talked like a tall Adolf Hitler, complete with mustache and walking with one hand behind his back. Who would want to get anywhere close to him, let alone get to know Him? As long as no rules were broken, things would be fine. But if you broke a rule, look out! That is the fearful misunderstanding I had about God, that I would only get His attention if I did something wrong. Doing something right did not incur His attention because I was *supposed* to do things right.

It is amazing when someone focuses so hard on *not* doing things wrong that they are more prone to do things wrong.

So how did this view affect my worship? When I came to bring my "sacrifice of praise," I would lay it at the altar and run. I had no desire to stay in God's presence. I had no desire to commune with Him.

At the root of who I am as a person is not staying where I feel I'm not accepted. I certainly never felt good enough for God, so I came to Him with the obligatory worship and quickly exited.

How do you think God felt about all this? How do you feel when you are misrepresented? When someone says you are someone you are not. Doesn't something rise up within you?

All God wanted was for me to come to Him "as I am," but in my head I was thinking about "all I could be" and how short I had fallen. Certainly God couldn't be very happy with me, and if He was not very happy with me, why in the world would I want to be anywhere close?

On top of that I came from a large family (ten children) and rarely got the attention of my father (good or bad), so my thoughts were that God had sooo many "children" that He would be too busy to spend any one-on-one time with me. As long as I kept myself busy and out of his hair, things would be fine.

> Fear of intimacy, whether for a man or woman, is usually founded in a lack of trust.

This thinking does not bode well for approaching God in worship. How would it sound if, in worship, I came to God saying, "Excuse me, I don't mean to bother you. I know you are busy and all, but . . ."? I dare say I would not find any intimacy in worship there.

And speaking of intimacy, how close is close? In a marriage relationship (which is symbolic of the relationship the Church has with God), you can have "a coming together" without intimacy, but it is very difficult to have intimacy without "a coming together" (whatever that coming together might look like).

Fear of intimacy, whether for a man or woman, is usually founded in a lack of trust. If one does not have a trust relationship with God where you can look into His eyes and feel vulnerable and safe at the same time, you will not have intimacy, and your worship of God will be forever hindered and less than what God has designed it to be.

I have just touched on a few examples of how our view of God affects our worship.

I'm sure you will come up with a whole lot more.

All I would ask is that you run everything through the filter of relationship with God. Anything that keeps you from drawing closer to Him in worship is an enemy of your soul.

Address it, deal with it, get it out of the way, and move in closer to the heart of God. It is there, close to God's heart, that you will find fulfillment, a resting place, and sense of getting back to your original design.

Discussion:

1. How close are you comfortable with in approaching God in worship?
2. Describe a time when you connected with God during worship. What did you think, feel?
3. When you close your eyes during worship, what image of God do you see?
4. How do you respond to the word "intimacy" when it comes to worship?
5. What does God get out of your worship?

Action Plan:

Today I…

(This is what I learned.)

And I…

(This is how I will apply what I learned.)

CHAPTER 7

Prayer

How Does My View of God Affect My Prayer?

Again, as we take a look at how your view of God affects your prayer, take a piece of paper and draw a line down the middle of it. On the one column put at the top "Wrong view," and on the second column put "Result."

When I say "prayer," I am not saying "prayers." Prayer is a dialogue, interaction, speaking *and* listening. We have formalized prayer so much that it has taken the relationship part right out of it.

So when I ask, "How does your view of God affect your prayer," I am asking about the talking part, the communication part, the speaking and listening part.

Can I be so bold as to say if there is no relationship there is no prayer, only prayers? Who among us like one-way relationships? Methinks no one.

We need to find a way to think of God as a cognizant being with feelings and emotions and a desire for relationship and a heart to provide for His children. Once we get into that paradigm, then we can start the interaction.

So what is preventing you from that kind of interaction? I've already shared a bit from my background and how it has affected my worship. The distance I originally felt from God, the bigness, the sense He was busy with others—all those things affected my prayer life.

As I mentioned, I was raised in a large family of ten children. The part I have yet to say is that we were very poor. Being the fifth of five boys, I knew all too well the meaning of hand-me-downs. One thing you very seldom got in my family was something new.

> I thought life was all about what God wants, not about what Dan wants.

Something else you very seldom got in our home was your wants. Your needs were first on the list; if they were met, that was enough. When I first saw the verse in the Psalms that said, "Delight yourself in the Lord and He will give you the desires of your heart" (Ps. 37:5), it was very hard for me to grasp.

I asked the question aloud, "You mean God wants to meet more than just my needs but my desires as well?"

The last few years, God has been taking me on a journey in that direction. When I pray and ask God what His desire is in a certain situation, I have often heard Him say, "What do you want, Dan?"

That question caught me so off guard. I thought life was all about what God wants, not about what Dan wants.

That kind of thinking can be a breeding ground for resentment. You could think that life is about everyone else but not about you. To clarify, I am not suggesting a selfish life here.

I remind you that the first part of the verse says to delight ourselves in God. It is hard to delight yourself in God and be selfish at the same time.

There is a place, I believe, in relationship with our Heavenly Father where we can ask for our needs *and* our wants. After all, didn't Jesus say that He had come to us so that we might have life and that we might have it to the full (John 10:10)?

He did *not* say, "I have come that you might have life, a life of denial and lack. All that I have created is *not* for you to enjoy, so hands off. Abstain from all enjoyment. Embrace poverty and thereby embrace spirituality."

That just makes no sense to me. Anyone who thinks like that cannot be enjoying their relationship with God. Enduring it but not enjoying it.

Remember life is all about relationship with God. What kind of relationship is based on withholding? Now I am not saying we will get everything we ask for. There is the aspect of delayed gratification.

What I am saying, however, is that we don't ask for enough. In the book of James, there is an interesting statement, it says, "You have not because you ask not."

> So if I, an earthly father, can give good gifts to my children, how much more does our Heavenly Father want to provide for our needs *and* wants.

I have had many interesting experiences in life, things that others have desired for themselves. I was a guest on a national television sports program called *Off the Record* filmed in Toronto, Ontario, that had guests from all walks of life discussing sports-related issues.

When I returned to Ottawa, I was bombarded with the question, "How did you get on that program?" My response was so simple. I answered, "I asked!"

As a father, I am glad to be able to provide for my children. I love the look on my son or daughter's face when something they have asked for is presented to them.

They asked, and I took joy in providing it for them. So if I, an earthly father, can give good gifts to my children, how much more does our Heavenly Father want to provide for our needs *and* wants.

How has your view of God affected your prayer? Please spend some time getting in touch with what goes on inside you when it's time to pray or there is a need or desire to pray.

What are your instincts? Are they good (leading *to* God), or are they not so good, leading *away* from Him. They are both influenced by your relationship with God. Identify the influence, whether positive or negative, and deal with it appropriately.

The bottom line is that if God wants relationship with us, conversation must be part of that relationship. Make sense?

Discussion:

1. How do you react when I say prayer is a two-way conversation?
2. What would prevent *or* encourage you toward that kind of interaction?
3. When it comes to prayer, how has your relationship with your earthly father positively or negatively affected your prayer life?
4. How do you react when I say God is interested in your wants as well as your needs?

Action Plan:

Today I…

(This is what I learned.)

And I…

(This is how I will apply what I learned.)

CHAPTER 8

EVANGELISM

How Does My View of God Affect My Evangelism?

One more time, as we take a look at how your view of God affects your evangelism, take a piece of paper and draw a line down the middle of it. On the one column put at the top "Wrong view," and on the second column put "Result."

Why is it when someone preaches loud, they are called an evangelist, and when someone preaches quietly, they are called a teacher? It's something I've always wondered. I say this for a point, actually.

> If the world sees us as angry people, why would they be attracted to our message if they are not first attracted to us?

I was singing in Northern Alberta as part of an evangelistic crusade. I had finished my part of the program and was sitting with a young boy who was part of my host family.

As the "evangelist" started to speak, his voice began to rise, and he became quite demonstrative in his actions, pounding the pulpit from time to time.

The observant young boy leaned over and asked me the most profound question, "Why is that man so mad?"

That question really shook me. Actually, it really bothered me. It made me ask how we as Christians are being perceived by the world.

If the world sees us as angry people, why would they be attracted to our message if they are not first attracted to us?

I was getting gas the other day, and at another pump was a truck with posters and sayings that consumed its exterior. Upon closer examination, I read the words that were the reason for all this extreme publicity.

There were words such as, "Judgment is coming, are you ready," "You cannot escape judgment," and "God hates sin so repent!" I asked myself if this advertising for God would get me to buy the product or not. I thought not!

Who would want to approach such an angry, judgmental God?

> God the Father loves to draw people to Himself,
> to woo them by His Spirit.

I was reminded of the fire-and-brimstone preaching of a few years back (actually, more than a few!). Churches were full of guilt-ridden people who ran to the altar to escape hell. I ask you one question (and by asking, likely offending a lot of you): why are those churches no longer full?

Dare I say those that ran to the altar to escape hell thought they had received a free ticket to heaven but never found relationship with God?

Those that found relationship with God remained, but their numbers were much fewer than those the "revivalists" advertised. I wonder what God was thinking at the time.

It reminds me of when a family would come to visit another family. Both families happened to have kids about the same age. The host family would introduce the visitors and say to their children, "Now these are your new friends."

Sometimes it would work, and sometimes there was no natural connection. It was a bit forced, and no one likes forced friendship.

And neither does God.

God the Father loves to draw people to Himself, woo them by His Spirit. I dare say that God was not portrayed as a "lover" during those fire-and-brimstone times.

So in light of the question, "How does my view of God affect my evangelism?" we need to ask ourselves how we are communicating to those who do not know God, who God is.

I had the opportunity once when I was on tour as a Christian singer to meet and share with a German exchange student who had never even heard about God. What do you say to someone with a completely blank slate and no frame of reference?

We muddled through, and at the end of our discussion, she came away with a sense that there was something bigger than us (God) but didn't quite connect with the idea that He wanted a relationship with her.

Sad to say that is where most of the world is today—unaware that God is pursuing them. Someone needs to tell them the good news that the God who created them wants a relationship with them.

What if you were to take out a full page ad in your local newspaper to promote a relationship with God, what would you include? What would be your hook? What words would you use? Pictures?

We in North America have not done a very good job at "selling God" to the masses. More people have been turned off to God because of the church than turned toward Him because of the church.

As I previously mentioned, my brothers went through a terrible childhood of church abuse that made it very difficult for them to see God in any of the church. They mistakenly thought the church that was abusing them represented God. It did not!

Add to the mix faulty televangelists, insecure pastors, domineering lay leadership, and the never-ending church splits and it is easy to get a wrong message about God.

If I had one prayer about evangelism, it would be that each person would be able to experience God firsthand and then based on that experience make a decision whether or not to follow Him and enter into a relationship with Him.

After all, isn't evangelism not about bringing people to church but about introducing them to God, to the good news that they can have relationship with God?

Discussion:

1. How does the world view your evangelistic efforts/attempts?
2. Is there any merit to the statement that people must first be attracted to you before they will hear your message?
3. How did Jesus share his faith?
4. What part of God do people see when they observe your life?
5. With what ways are you comfortable sharing your faith?

Action Plan:

Today I…

(This is what I learned.)

And I…

(This is how I will apply what I learned.)

CHAPTER 9

DISCIPLESHIP

How Does My View of God Affect My Discipleship?

For the last time, as we take a look at how your view of God affects your discipleship, take a piece of paper and draw a line down the middle of it. On the one column put at the top "Wrong view," and on the second column put "Result."

When I say the word *discipleship*, I simply mean our relationship with each other as Christians but focusing more on leadership.

Our view of God filtered to us through our pastors and/or church leadership has greatly missed the mark.

Some of it flows up, as in a layperson relating to spiritual leadership. Some of it flows down, as in spiritual leadership relating to a layperson. And some of it is horizontal, flowing from brother to brother, sister to sister, etc.

Through the years, the church (God's "called out" people) has not been very good to each other. Instead of taking on God's nature and character, they have taken on some distorted personality that wounds the wounded and condemns the condemned.

Our view of God filtered to us through our pastors and/or church leadership has greatly missed the mark. I am not saying that all pastors and church leadership are faulty. What I am saying is that most wrong views of God come from some form of faulty church leadership.

A phrase was coined a few years back that talked about servant leadership. This leadership was modeled after Jesus, who came not to be served but to serve. In my mind, I thought that maybe we were finally getting it. Church leadership was intended to serve and not be served.

And yet we still see church leadership in their ivory towers, distanced from their flock, in some cases lording it over their flock as a ruler in his kingdom. Something is wrong with that. There is an improper view of God here.

I've heard it said that power corrupts and absolute power corrupts absolutely. Many leaders in the church have separated themselves from the flock and their own leadership by making everyone accountable to them.

With this position of authority, many church leaders have lost their smell of sheep.

They feel they have been called to the mountain like Moses and have been placed in irrefutable leadership. However, they are not accountable to anyone. That is absolute power.

They say they are accountable to God only, but that is not even true. If it were true, why would they treat the sheep like they do, like pawns in a chess game or foot soldiers in a battle?

This separation from the sheep and all other authority has led many church leaders into sin and stained the view of God's church by many who might look to the church for refuge.

Where does this thinking come from? It starts with a wrong view of God.

If you were to view God as a tyrant, someone without feeling and task oriented, you might deal with your flock the same way. If you viewed God as high above and you way below, that also would influence how you view and treat the flock God has given you.

If you viewed God as the taskmaster who was waiting for you to do something wrong so He could slap your wrist, that too would affect your leadership style in the church.

As previously stated, all these wrong views of God are fueled by one thing and one thing only: fear.

If you viewed God as a results-only coach who only affirmed you when you accomplished something, then you might convey that thinking to your congregation by only affirming them if they did something noticeable but ignored them or even derided them if they failed.

If you viewed God as one who was waiting at the finish line to bring up all the things you did wrong, that view would permeate your interaction with others with a sense they would never be good enough.

Are you catching my drift?

All these wrong views of God are fueled by one thing and one thing only: fear. In my rigid upbringing, to fear God was to be afraid of Him. That was so wrong. It was much later that I learned that to fear God was to have a "reverential trust."

Fear's natural instinct is to protect oneself. If we have a wrong fear of God, we will endeavor in our relationships with others and especially in our leadership of others ultimately to try to protect ourselves.

The opposite of fear is trust.

That is why leaders try to insulate themselves by ascending to their ivory towers, or at the very least gather a bunch of yes-men around them so that their leadership will never be challenged.

That's why wrong leadership is consumed with control because then they can determine the outcome of every meeting and determine their own destiny. They fear losing control and will do everything within their power, whether godly or ungodly, to maintain that control.

Again, the opposite of fear is trust. It's like the old saying, "In God we trust, all others pay cash." Only in this leadership setting not even God is trusted.

If someone does not trust God, they will not trust others. If someone does not fear God appropriately, they will not fear others. If someone does not love God the way that he is loved by God, he will not love others.

All this is a journey, and to be sure, there are no perfect leaders in the church. Neither are there perfect sheep. Once you get to that place of humility, you can begin the journey to servant leadership.

We all fear. We all do the same things in varying degrees until we find our rest in God. The most attractive leadership to be around is the one that is settled in his proper view of God and himself. It is to that end we must put our efforts.

How I treated other Christians was really how I was treating God.

The scripture says to "labor to enter the rest that there is for the people of God." Dare I say so boldly that wrong leadership has not entered that rest, that place where no matter what they do or do not do, they are okay with God.

Sometimes we need others to point this out for us. That is true discipleship. If you don't know your heart is broken, how can you fix it?

The bottom line is, how we view God determines how we treat others.

When God revealed to me that the body of Christ was not just an entity in Christendom but that the body of Christ was the *body of Christ*, that changed my view. How I treated other Christians was really how I was treating God.

You see it's all connected, interwoven if you'd like. Our right view of God is essential for life here on earth, for a fruitful life here on earth.

How's your view of God, and how is it affecting your relationships within the body of Christ? Take a moment and ask God to show you how you may have treated others improperly based on your wrong view of Him.

There may need to be some forgiveness asked *and* given. After all, once we start loving each other as God loved us, then we will be giving the world a proper view of God.

Discussion:

1. How would a wrong view of God cause leadership to wound the wounded or condemn the condemned?
2. Have you been improperly wounded or condemned by church leadership or other Christians? Discuss it.
3. What, in your view, is servant leadership?
4. How do you see leadership in the body of Christ?
5. What wrong view of God has wrongly affected your interaction in the body of Christ?

Action Plan:

Today I…

(This is what I learned.)

And I…

(This is how I will apply what I learned.)

CHAPTER 10

END OF DAYS

Whoever started the rumor that at the end of our lives God is going to play a video of our lives, all the good *and* bad (especially the bad), needs to be strung up by their eyelids and forced to blink. What a horrendous thought! What a horrendous lie!

For God to review all our past sins would mean He would have to deny Himself, deny His own character, deny His own words. Didn't He say that "our sins and iniquities will I remember no more"?

> The anxiety and apprehension of standing before a holy God dissipate now that I know of God's intentions.

If He is indeed a God of His word, the sins we have confessed and asked forgiveness for are forgiven and wiped from His memory. At that day, we will stand before God not in our own righteousness but the righteous of God's Son, Jesus.

There indeed is someone who reminds us of our past sins, but it is not God. His name is the "accuser of the brethren," the devil. He will do whatever is within his power to have us not look forward to seeing God for the first time face-to-face.

I once had planned to cower in God's presence when I stood before Him in judgment, but now I know I can approach His throne of grace boldly because "when He looks at me He sees not what I used to be but He sees Jesus."

Maybe that is another thing the apostle Paul meant when he said death has no more sting. The fear of judgment is gone. The anxiety and apprehension of standing before a holy God dissipate now that I know of God's intentions.

God's intentions are to welcome us home, to say to us, "Well done, you good and faithful servant." Isn't that something for which to look forward?

Instead of fearing reprisal for any wrong you committed on earth, what if you anticipated God saying "thanks" for choosing to be in a relationship with Him.

My understanding of all this might be a little different than most. Check this out. The apostle Paul talks about meeting God in 1 Corinthians 3.

The picture I see is when we die and stand before God, a fire will come and burn all the works we have done on earth, good or bad. What survives this holy fire will be gold, silver, and brass, those works motivated by God's Holy Spirit and responded to by us.

> People choose to go to hell by rejecting God's gift of salvation.

At that point, we gather our "crowns" and present them to God, who at that time will say "thanks." That part of Scripture says that some might not have a lot of crowns to present but at the very least will be saved "so as by fire."

For the unbeliever, there will indeed be judgment because they have not dealt with their sin (that which separates them from relationship with God). In not dealing with their sin, they have chosen to reject the offer of salvation.

I made a statement once that shook a lot of people. It went like this, "God sends no one to hell!" Of course, everyone within earshot was aghast until I completed my thought, "People choose to go to hell by rejecting God's gift of salvation."

People are not sent to hell; they choose to go to hell. Big difference. God's heart is that everyone would be saved, but that is sadly not the case. Because He gives us the choice, the responsibility is ours. And some will make the wrong choice.

If you are reading this book and have not yet decided to enter in to relationship with God, now would be a great time. This is what you do:

1. Realize God wants relationship with you.
2. Realize your sins block that relationship.
3. Ask God to forgive your sins so you can be in a relationship with Him.
4. Thank Him for coming to live in you, for befriending you, for saying He would now never leave you or forsake you.

When you pray this prayer, God will come and live in your life. He will be as close as your breath. He will want to continue this relationship that has just started and want it to go deeper, further.

You have never met anyone quite like God—the real God, the God who created the earth, put man in the Garden of Eden for a relationship. Adam broke that relationship and was told to leave the Garden of Eden.

God then sent His son to restore that relationship. Jesus had to die to conquer the sin that stood between us and God, but He did it out of a heart of love and in response to a heart of love—the love of His Father.

Most of you reading this book will already be in some sort of relationship with God. You are reading this book to be in "better" relationship with God.

Make your best effort to lay aside the things that would keep you from drawing closer to your Father God.

He wants to reveal more of His character and nature to you. Up till now, some of you have put up walls, but today is your chance to slowly bring those walls down.

As previously mentioned, fear is the absence of trust. One of my favorite Bible verses is found in 1 John 4, where it says that "Perfect (mature) love casts out all fear."

> I would rather meet Him with the anticipation of reuniting with a great friend than the anticipation of some kind of harsh judgment.

If you could find a way to cautiously expose your heart to God's love, you will find your fear dissipating. It won't all happen overnight, but it will be an incredible journey.

So often we have made Christianity about the destination (heaven) and have lost the joy of the journey. To use a trite saying, "Smelling the roses along the way" or, as I would prefer to say, "Enjoying a relationship with God along the way."

Someday we will all meet God. I would rather meet Him with the anticipation of reuniting with a great friend than the anticipation of some kind of harsh judgment. I would rather feel like I am coming home where I am safe.

What about you?

Discussion:

1. What was/is your view of the "end of days" when you die and face God?
2. What were/are your fears regarding the coming meeting with God?
3. How would you live differently if you were awaiting thanks instead of judgment?

Action Plan:

Today I…

(This is what I learned.)

And I…

(This is how I will apply what I learned.)

IN CLOSING

When I was in my early teens, I would have a recurring dream that I had died, and I wasn't sure if I was going to heaven or hell. Often I would wake up in a sweat and with a sense of panic.

Then I gave my life wholly to God, holding nothing back. Soon after, I had a dream where I saw Jesus returning for His church, and I had absolute confidence that I was one of them.

From that day to this, I have slept with confidence that whether I live or die, I will never leave God's presence.

The following song comes out of reflecting on that experience. At first, I am an observer in this great heavenly environment and then a participant.

What joy! What unspeakable joy to know I will be there with the millions worshipping the One who loved me so much.

Would you join me?

    And We Cried Holy
    Dan Thiessen © 1998

    Verse One:

    And I heard a sound in Heaven,
    The sound of many waters to my ears
    As I gazed upon the host of Heaven,
    I saw them rise as Christ the Lamb appeared

    CHORUS:

    And they cried Holy, Holy, Holy is the Lamb
    And they cried Holy, Holy, Holy is the Lamb

Verse Two:

Around the throne were four and twenty elders
And then I saw the ones who'd gone before
Again the song began to roll like thunder
I asked the Lord if He could show me more

Bridge:

And then I looked around this scene from Heaven
Suddenly I came to realize,
That there I was, joining in the chorus
I'd been redeemed, now Heaven filled my eyes

CHORUS:

And we cried Holy, Holy, Holy is the Lamb,
And we cried Holy, Holy, Holy is the Lamb

ABOUT THE AUTHOR

Dan Thiessen hails from British Columbia, Canada. He has travelled from coast to coast in Canada and the United States, Northern Ireland, and Scotland, visiting churches of nearly every major denomination both as a singer/songwriter, worship leader, and speaker.

His message has always been the same, which is why he was able to cross so many denominational lines: Who we perceive God to be determines how close we get to Him.

Dan's desire is for every person to have their own experience with God. This study was written with that in mind.

Dan has written hundreds of songs (a worship song recorded by Christ for the Nations in Dallas, Texas), a weekly article in a newspaper for two years, a number of e-books and is published in a compendium of short stories together with Corrie ten Boom and Max Lucado called Heart of a Father.

You can contact Dan at: dan@danthiessen.com.

Also by Dan Thiessen:

Safe Place
Father's Heart Devotional

CPSIA information can be obtained
at www.ICGtesting.com
Printed in the USA
LVHW04s0734180718
584013LV00001B/62/P